The Invitation

Why Are You Here?
When Will You Respond?
Do You Control Time?

I wish I had known God earlier.

Kakra Baiden

Contents

Chapter 1

The Invitation

RSVP

It was one of the most beautiful wedding invitations I had ever received. The card itself was large, A4 size. When I opened it, I discovered seven other invitation cards. Apart from the main wedding invitation, there were other invitations cards to participate in a dinner, a photo shoot, a cocktail party, plus other events, which spanned a period of about two days. At the foot of the main card was an RSVP with the number and name of someone you were supposed to call to confirm whether you would respond to the various invitations or not.

RSVP is an abbreviation of a French phrase: *Répondez s'il vous plaît.* It means to please respond to an invitation.

From the time you are born to the time you die, you will receive several different invitations, but there is a peculiar invitation you must respond positively to. This peculiar spiritual invitation is called the invitation of God, or the call of God.

The Call of God Means the Invitation of God

You may ask, what invitation is this? It's an invitation from God Himself. This invitation is also described in the Bible as the call of God. The call simply means, an invitation. I will be using both terms interchangeably in this book. It's a spiritual invitation, and whether you are aware or not, God has sent you an invitation, and you need to respond positively to it.

What's the Ultimate Purpose of This Invitation?

"And we know that in all things God works for the good of those who love him, who have been called according to his purpose. For those God foreknew he also predestined to be conformed to the image of his Son, that he might be the first-born among many brothers and sisters. And those he predestined, he also called; those he called, he also justified; those he justified, he also glorified. What, then, shall we say in response to these things? If God is for us, who can be against us? He who did not spare his own Son, but gave him up for us all—how will he not also, along with him, graciously give us all things?" (Romans 8:28-32).

Every Invitation Has a Purpose

I remember the first time I invited my wife out to dinner. I had previously tried to arrange it with a friend of mine, Esinam, who failed in this assignment. At the next attempt I did it myself, and I finally succeeded. Since I invited her, I determined the purpose of the invitation. The invitee determines the purpose of every invitation. That's why God calls or invites us "according to his purpose" or plan.

The purpose of this plan is to be "conformed to the image of his Son." "For those God foreknew he also predestined to be conformed to the image of his Son." To conform means to be similar to, and image means exact likeness. In short, when we are conformed into the image of His Son, we become similar to the exact likeness of Jesus.

This may surprise some, but the ultimate purpose of the call of God is not to preach. Preaching is a means to an end, not an end in itself. God did not create man to preach; He created man in His image so he could have dominion.

Should You Be Bothered About the Call of God?

You may say, what has being conformed to the image of Jesus got to do with me? I have bills to pay and I have my own plans; I am not interested in this. There are certain things in life that have an impact on you, irrespective of whether you are interested, aware, or unaware.

For example: The tax man makes plans with your income without consulting you. He does not bother to find out if you are planning a holiday or paid your bills. Failure to pay your taxes can land you in jail. Not being interested in taxes does not make you immune from its consequences. In the same way, a failure to positively RSVP this invitation will have serious consequences on you in time and eternity.

What Is Life All About?

Have you ever had a hollow feeling in your heart about the futility of life? I once engaged a dying multimillionaire in a conversation. As he was approaching death, he felt he had overworked, and everything he had achieved was not that important. His main interests were: right relationships with people, and preparing his heart to meet God.

Imagine you went to bed one day and miraculously woke up in a paradise where everything you ever wished for was available at your beck and call. You may enjoy the place, but there will always be a void in your heart and a question on your mind: *Why am I here?*

Why are you on this earth, who brought you here, could life be better, is there something you are supposed to be doing, and what happens when you die? The answers to these questions lie in your response to the call or invitation of God. You have been invited, and it has repercussions on you in time and eternity. You must respond to the invitation!

Types of Responses

1. You can have a cynical response to this invitation.

I once spoke to a man who had never heard about the call of God. He told me he believed in science because he could prove it. His main interest was the pleasures of life. He reminded me of the cynical response of some people to the call of God in the book of Isaiah:

"But see, there is joy and revelry, slaughtering of cattle and killing of sheep, eating of meat and drinking of wine! 'Let us eat and drink,' you say, 'for tomorrow we die!' " (Isaiah 22:13).

2. You can have a nonchalant response to this invitation.

My friend Stephen was a committed Christian when I first got to know him. He was so interested in God's plan for his life. As life progressed and he made more money and had more opportunities, he started cooling off towards the things of God. Finally he lost almost all interest. His response to the call became nonchalant, which means he relaxed and did not care much about the invitation anymore. His attitude reminded me of one of Paul's trusted aides who backslid:

"for Demas, because he loved this world, has deserted me and has gone to Thessalonica. Crescens has gone to Galatia, and Titus to Dalmatia" (2 Timothy 4:10).

3. You must have the right response.

You and I must be like Paul, aggressive in our response to the call. He was prepared to fight to finish his race or God's plan for his life:

"I have fought the good fight, I have finished the race, I have kept the faith" (2 Timothy 4:7).

Conforming to the Image of Jesus: What Is the Image of His Son?

I remember the first time I went to the States and tried buying a pair of trousers. The sales assistant asked me if I liked the pants over there. I was expecting to see underwear, but I saw trousers. I was confused. I did not know trousers were called pants. Words can mean different things, depending on location and context. For example, a mouse in computing is not a literal mouse, it's a pointing device.

When you read, image of His Son, your mind will naturally gravitate towards a photo of Jesus. The image of Jesus is quite different from image as you know it. Let's explore it.

I Saw Jesus in a Trance

I remember the first time I saw Jesus in a trance. I was praying at dawn on the rooftop of my father's house. Suddenly I felt a mighty presence all around me. I started running away, but when I got to the door, I couldn't raise my hand to open it because flesh rebelled against command. My hand froze.

I saw the heavens open and the whole world seemed to light up. I saw Jesus descending from heaven. I fell on my knees and started pleading that He would not kill me. He was very huge and His head touched the clouds. He looked like a person made out of very bright light.

What Did Paul See When He Saw Jesus?

Paul had a similar experience on the road to Damascus. This was his account:

"On one of these journeys I was going to Damascus with the authority and commission of the chief priests. About noon, King Agrippa, as I was on the road, I saw a light from heaven, brighter than the sun, blazing around me and my companions. We all fell to the ground, and I heard a voice saying to me in Aramaic, 'Saul, Saul, why do you persecute me? It is hard for you to kick against the goads.' "Then I asked, 'Who are you, Lord?' " 'I am Jesus, whom you are persecuting,' the Lord replied" (Acts 26:12-15).

I want you to notice how he described the image he saw, "As I was on the road I saw a light." He saw an image made out of light.

I remember asking Jesus, "Why do You shine so much?" He said, "That is the colour of holiness; it emits a light." It made me understand the verse, "God is light." It seems God is "made up of holiness," and holiness shines in the spirit realm as light.

Look at how John described God:

"God is light, and in him is no darkness at all" (1 John 1:5).

I believe the image of God is the visible reflection of His attributes, and holiness is the main feature of the image of God. God is holy.

**Why Must I Be Conformed to
the Image of His Son?**

**1. It was God's initial purpose for
creating man.**

Sometimes when I see chickens on a farm I
feel sad for them because they are totally oblivious of the primary reason why they are on the
farm. They may think they are just enjoying free
boarding and lodging and to have pleasure. What
they don't know is that the farmer has an ultimate purpose: to turn them into food. Their ignorance or disinterest does not change the purpose
of the farmer.

God stated His plan for creating man clearly
at creation. He said, "Let us make man in our
image, after our likeness: and let them have
dominion" (Genesis 1:26).

2. It is God's end purpose for saving man.

My son asked me a question recently. He said,
"What will be our age when we get to heaven?
Will we be old or young?" I gave him an intelligent guess. I said, "I suspect around thirty."
"Why?" he asked. I quoted this Scripture from the
book of John:

"Dear friends, now we are children of God, and
what we will be has not yet been made known.
But we know that when Christ appears, we shall

13

be like him, for we shall see him as he is. All who have this hope in him purify themselves, just as he is pure" (1 John 3:2-3).

John said we don't have complete knowledge about how we will look, but "we shall be like Him," or be conformed to His image when we see him, Jesus.

Jesus was resurrected when He was around thirty years old. That's why I believe we shall be around that age, because after all, we shall be like Him. After this, we will reign or have dominion as kings together with Him.

"And hast made us unto our God kings and priests: and we shall reign on the earth" (Revelation 5:10, KJV).

I want us to examine in more detail why we must be conformed to the image of His Son.

Chapter 2

Fellowship with God

"God is faithful, who has called you into fellowship with his Son, Jesus Christ our Lord" (1 Corinthians 1:9).

Why I Couldn't Fellowship with Rocky

I once had a dog called Rocky. I wanted to train it to be indoors. Because of this I used to bring it to my bedroom to fellowship with me. One day it lay on its back and started urinating on my carpet. I became frustrated and decided to keep it outdoors. The dog was refusing to behave like me, so the fellowship ceased.

The Image of God Makes Fellowship Possible

Generally we tend to hang out or fellowship with people who are like us. That's why Christians, athletes, film stars, and even crooks tend to hang out with each other. That's why we must have the image of God, to fellowship with Him.

When Adam hadn't sinned, he could talk to God face-to-face and enjoy fellowship with Him because before the fall of man he looked like Him. It's interesting that even within species, communication is restricted to "image." You must be a bird to communicate effectively with other birds.

Sin Corrupted Man's Image and Disrupted Fellowship

When my children were younger, they would run to me with open arms anytime I came back from work and I would lift them up, throw them up and down, and finally hug them. The only thing that disrupted this fellowship was when they had soiled themselves. I would suddenly smell something and say, "Uuuh." I would put them down and tell them to go and have a bath. Sin makes you smell and disrupts fellowship with God.

One day as usual God came to fellowship with Adam:

"The LORD God called to the man, 'Where are you?' He answered, 'I heard you in the garden, and I was afraid because I was naked; so I hid' " (Genesis 3:9-10).

Adam ran away because of sin. Sin corrupted his image and broke the fellowship. To corrupt means to add or remove something. When you add salt or remove the gas from a bottle of soda, you have corrupted it.

In a recount of the fall of Adam, Paul said:

"But I fear, lest by any means, as the serpent beguiled Eve through his subtilty, so your minds should be corrupted from the simplicity that is in Christ" (2 Corinthians 11:3, KJV).

That is why " all have sinned and fall short of the glory of God" (Romans 3:23).

Even on earth we must have a semblance of His image to fellowship with Him. John said.

"If we claim to have fellowship with him and yet walk in the darkness, we lie and do not live out the truth. But if we walk in the light, as he is in the light, we have fellowship with one another, and the blood of Jesus, his Son, purifies us from all sin" (1 John 1:6-7).

3

Chapter 3

Dominion

"And God said, Let us make man in our image, after our likeness: and let them have dominion" (Genesis 1:26, KJV).

The Image of God Gave Man Dominion

To have dominion means to reign or rule. There seems to be a correspondence between image and dominion. In the movie *The Planet of the Apes*, apes started having dominion over humans because their brains developed. Their "image changed." The main reason why humans have dominion over animals is because of the size of their brain. This unique characteristic about our image makes us dominate animals. Before the fall of man, Adam's unique image made him have dominion. What kind of dominion did man have? Let's examine them.

1. The image of God gave man dominion over poverty.

Sometime back a friend of mine came to see me for prayer. When I saw him I thought he was suffering from cancer, HIV, or some other dangerous disease. Finally I got to know he was not sick but in debt. Debt can make a healthy man sick. One of the blessings of the Lord is to be debt free, "You will lend to many nations but will borrow from none" (Deuteronomy 28:12).

Before the fall of man, Adam did not have debts; a mortgage, heating bills, or unpaid credit card bills. Because everything was free, he had dominion over poverty.

"And the LORD God commanded the man, "You are free to eat from any tree in the garden" (Genesis 2:16).

2. The image of God gave man dominion over the devil.

I have personally witnessed the devil oppress the children of God. I once prayed over a bottle of anointing oil for a man whose sick wife had been bedridden for five years. When he got home, he anointed his wife with the oil. He told me his wife started manifesting in the bed as the evil spirits left. The next morning his wife had been completely healed. Praise be to Jesus!

Something like this could not have happened to Adam before the fall. The devil could not afflict him with a disease or tempt him to be unfaithful to his spouse. Adam had dominion over the devil. It was only when he sinned that he became vulnerable. The Lord said to him,

"And I will put enmity between you and the woman, and between your offspring and hers; he will crush your head, and you will strike his heel" (Genesis 3:15).

From that time, man became vulnerable to the devil. He could bruise or attack man.

3. The image of God gave man dominion over the "flesh."

Flesh that is out of control is a dangerous thing. Marriages have been destroyed and homes broken because of fleshy impulses that cannot be controlled.

A married man once told me he had an insatiable desire for prostitutes. He could not concentrate until he had an affair with a prostitute. He had to do it regularly. It badly affected his marriage.

In the beginning, Adam dominated his flesh because it was not corrupted. When he fell, the nature of his flesh changed. This corrupted man's flesh and gave birth to "the works of the flesh," as described in the Bible. One of the categories of the works of the flesh is sexual sins.

"The acts of the flesh are obvious: sexual immorality, impurity and debauchery" (Galatians 5:19).

When a man becomes born again, his sprit is recreated, but his corrupted flesh remains the same. The flesh has to be controlled by the Spirit; otherwise you will live in sin.

4. The image of God gave man dominion over sin and death.

One day I went to a hospital to visit a member of mine who was in intensive care. He was dying of HIV. As I stood by his emaciated body, I remembered the countless times I had warned him about his immoral lifestyle. Sadly he died shortly after. Sin always leads to death.
God warned Adam,

"but you must not eat from the tree of the knowledge of good and evil, for when you eat from it you will certainly die" (Genesis 2:17).

When Adam sinned, he became a victim of both physical and spiritual death.
When my dad died, his body lay lifeless on the bed because his spirit had been separated from his body. However, I believe he did not suffer spiritual death because he died as a Christian. I believe he is in heaven with the Lord.
Physical death is the separation of the spirit from the body. Spiritual death is the separation of the spirit from God.

5. The image of God will lead to the restoration of all things.

"and that he may send the Messiah, who has been appointed for you—even Jesus. Heaven must receive him until the time comes for God to restore everything, as he promised long ago through his holy prophets since the world began" (Acts 3:20-21).

The Meaning of Restoration

Restoration means to restore that which was lost or stolen to its proper owner. One day someone stole my iPad and other items of mine. Through "find" on my iPad, the police were able to track the thief and recover the iPad and the items. I received restitution.

Peter preached a powerful sermon to the people that gathered after healing a lame man. I want you to notice what he said about Jesus concerning restoration.

After his ascension to heaven, "heaven must receive him (Jesus) until the time comes for God to restore everything" This restoration will include the image of God.

Chapter 4

How the Call of God Works

The Call

The call is made up of a series of invitations from God. As we respond to these invitations, we are progressively and incrementally changed into His image. These invitations are made by the Holy Spirit at a time and place of His choosing and interwoven with everyday life. There is usually no fanfare accompanying the different invitations, although some people may have a supernatural experience. Consider Jesus's invitation to His disciples to follow Him. It was an ordinary day and they were going about their normal fishing business when Jesus invited them to follow Him. This is what happened.

"As Jesus was walking beside the Sea of Galilee, he saw two brothers, Simon called Peter and his brother Andrew. They were casting a net into the lake, for they were fishermen. 'Come, follow me,' Jesus said, 'and I will send you out to fish for people.' At once they left their nets and followed him" (Matthew 4:18-20).

A Means to an End

The call of God is a means to an end. It's not an end in itself. Means is something you do to achieve something, and the end is the reason why you are doing what you are doing. Sometimes we can become so focused on the means that we forget about the end.

Sometimes when I officiate weddings I think about all the effort that goes into the ceremony; the cakes, the reception, the flower girls, the venue, etc. All these are good, but they represent the means to the marriage, not the end.

Married people must be more concerned about being faithful to each other, which is more of the end; but how little effort is made in that direction. More effort is put into the means than the end.

When you say the call of God, the average Christians mind tends to think about the work of the ministry. This is part of the call, but not all of it. You must, however, remember the call simply means an invitation, and every invitation has a specific purpose. The end purpose is to be conformed to the image of His Son.

There Are Many Calls

If you study the Bible carefully, you will notice there are many calls. A failure to understand the multiplicity of calls will lead to a disproportionate

focus on one call at the expense of equally important ones. This can lead to a distorted image.

The call of God is a transformational process
that starts in eternity, extends into time, and
terminates in eternity. Its ultimate purpose is
to transform us into the image of His Son. Let's
trace its progress from eternity into time and
back to eternity.

The Call of God Starts from Eternity

I remember when my first daughter, Phoebe,
was born. She was born under miraculous
circumstances. At that time I was a final-year
architectural student and my wife was a final-
year medical student. We took all necessary
precautions to avoid conception, but my wife still
managed to conceive. I was surprised.

Through ultrasound I knew she would be a
girl. I even saw her heartbeat. I knew her on
a screen before she was born. If I could know
her before she existed. it's not strange that the
almighty God knows all about us even before we
are born.

God knew Jeremiah before he was born. That's
why God said to Jeremiah,

"Before I formed you in the womb I knew you,
before you were born I set you apart; I appointed
you as a prophet to the nations" (Jeremiah 1:5).

God knew Jeremiah in eternity; that is, before time, and this applies to every human being. According to Paul, this detailed plan of every human life was drawn before the world begun. Amazing, and what depth of planning! The same concept is found in Paul's letter to Timothy:

"He has saved us and called us to a holy life—not because of anything we have done but because of his own purpose and grace. This grace was given us in Christ Jesus before the beginning of time" (2 Timothy 1:9).

This purpose or plan was drawn "before the beginning of time."

My greatest worry was my wife's expected delivery date. It was right in the middle of her final exams. I prayed to the Lord to give my wife strength to write her exams and also for the baby to be born on a weekend. She was born on Sunday night, and the following day my wife went on to write her next paper. She graduated without any issues. I thank God for His power.

The Call Is Based on God's Foreknowledge

Foreknowledge means to know something in advance.

"For those God foreknew he also predestined to be conformed to the image of his Son, that he might be the firstborn among many brothers and sisters" (Romans 8:29).

Before my daughter was born, I knew she would be a girl. I chose her name, Phoebe, from the Bible. Phoebe was the one who carried Paul's letter to the Romans. We made preparations and bought things in anticipation of her birth.

If I could have such foreknowledge, can you imagine God's foreknowledge about us? He knew your temperament, your social status, your race, gender, problems, strengths and weaknesses, finances, etc., even before you were born.

The book of Psalms also makes us understand that God has a book where He records the details of every human life long before it begins.

"My frame was not hidden from you when I was made in the secret place, when I was woven together in the depths of the earth. Your eyes saw my unformed body; all the days ordained for me were written in your book before one of them came to be" (Psalm 139:15-16).

God Predestines Every Life

Predestined means already determined. Based on the foreknowledge of our daughter's sex and expected date of delivery, we started making plans concerning her life. We even registered her in the preschool she would attend. We made plans concerning her based on our foreknowledge. God makes plans for our lives based on His foreknowledge about us.

"For those God foreknew he also predestined to be conformed to the image of his Son" (Romans 8:29).

He takes all He knows about us into consideration and designs a suitable plan for our life. For example, fishes are specially designed to live in water and birds are designed to fly. Don't look to men for validation; look to the Word and the Spirit of God. You are designed to succeed in your assignment.

Do We Have Free Will?

The next logical question will be, if everything is predestined, then does it mean we have no control over our choices and what we do?

I want you to notice, the word is qualified. We are predestined to "conform to the image of His Son"; not go to hell or something else; it's specific. This means God has already determined the course of our lives in order for us to conform to the image of His Son. We will have to make choices consistent with His will so this eternal purpose can be achieved.

When the choices we make, like the person we marry, the job we do, where we live, and what we do, is consistent with His will. Even the mundane experiences, whether good or bad, are designed to help us conform to the image of His Son.

My daughter Phoebe is now in university, but I predestined the course of her life towards that purpose. I took her to school, paid the fees, and saved for her college education. I had predetermined it; but it was still up to her to make choices consistent with my plans.

The Example of Moses

Take Moses, for example. God knew that someone with a slave mentality could not be a deliverer, so he raised him in Pharaoh's palace. Moses could not be intimidated like the other Israelites because

"Moses was educated in all the wisdom of the Egyptians and was powerful in speech and action" (Acts 7:22).

He was forced to go into exile for forty years, and that helped prepare him to be a shepherd for God's people. He tended the sheep of Jethro, a Midianite priest. Although everything looked like happenstance, there was a divine hand weaving the plan of God. Eventually his experiences transformed him more into the image of God. At a point, the Lord said to Moses, "See, I have made you like God to Pharaoh, and your brother Aaron will be your prophet" (Exodus 7:1). God said, "He has become like Me."

There is an invisible hand working out your life. Trust in God and be faithful to Him, because "the one who calls you is faithful, and he will do it" (1 Thessalonians 5:24).

Chapter 5

The Benefits of Responding to the Call of God

**The call makes "all things work,"
or brings comprehensive blessings.**

Man was blessed at the beginning of creation, and the call sets you on the path of blessings. Sometimes all you need to do to succeed at many things is to get one thing right. For example, a good education and skill can provide you with a good income, a car, a nice wedding, accommodations, and a comfortable life.

In this scenario, all you need to do is to get your education, right? Then all the other things I mentioned will begin to work or succeed. When a man chooses the call of God, it has a ripple effect on everything: his health, finances, peace, relationships, marriage, and even eternity.

"And we know that in all things God works for the good of those who love him, who have been called according to his purpose" (Romans 8:28)

It does not mean you will not have challenges, or you will be insulated from the problems of this world. You surely will, but the good, the bad, and the ugly will all work out for your good.

The call of God makes your positive and negative experiences work to your advantage.

Sometimes when food is being prepared, opposite ingredients are added. Something sweet like sugar can be added to something acidic like salt, but eventually everything works our for good. It produces good food.

Joseph was sold into slavery and framed, but eventually it rather led to his promotion as governor of Egypt. He said to his brothers,

"You intended to harm me, but God intended it for good to accomplish what is now being done, the saving of many lives" (Genesis 50:20).

That's why "we know that in all things God works for the good of those who love him, who have been called according to his purpose" (Romans 8:28).

All things means the good, the bad, and the ugly. What a blessing. That's one more reason why you must respond to the invitations. Imagine all aspects of your life—marriage, kids, ministry, finances, health, and eternity—all calibrated to form a perfect mix to the glory of God. This success is based on some factors I want us to consider.

The grace of God is connected to the call of God.

In preparation for the birth of my daughter, we provided what she would need once she was born. She did not have to work for anything; she enjoyed everything freely. There was a free car to take her home from the hospital. There was free accommodation and a bed. There was a cot, diapers, and feeding bottles, all freely provided. She enjoyed grace or help because we had planned for her.

When you are in God's plans, He will provide you with all you need for the plan to succeed. He will provide a marital partner, finances, friends, finances, and the anointing that is needed to carry out His plan. This is what Timothy had to say about the relationship between God's plan and grace:

"He has saved us and called us to a holy life—not because of anything we have done but because of his own purpose and grace. This grace was given us in Christ Jesus before the beginning of time" (2 Timothy 1:9).

I want you to notice that the grace and plan of God are coupled together. He who follows God's plans will discover His grace. "He that spared not his own Son, but delivered him up for us all, how shall he not with him also freely give us all things?" (Romans 8:32, KJV).

Your protection is linked to the call of God.

When my daughter was born, she remained indoors for a while, and we protected her from anything that would harm her. In the same way, God protects His plans. When I talk about protection, I mean spiritual and physical protection.

"What, then, shall we say in response to these things? If God is for us, who can be against us?" (Romans 8:31, KJV).

When the Pharisees wanted to persecute the disciples, Gamaliel, one of the Pharisees, warned them about the futility of fighting God's plan. He said,

Therefore, in the present case I advise you: Leave these men alone! Let them go! For if their purpose or activity is of human origin, it will fail. But if it is from God, you will not be able to stop these men; you will only find yourselves fighting against God" (Acts 5:38-39).

Are We Robots?

Does this mean we are supposed to be like robots and not make any plans of our own? Or are we all supposed to be priests? Not exactly.

Imagine I send my child to school. I sent him primarily to learn, but he can make friends, take up some sport, or go for a school party. My initial plan does not take away his free will to do other things.

All he needs to do is not to sacrifice my primary plan for other things. If he does, he will lose my financial support and help. In the same way, God gives us free will and some leverage, but we must never forget His eternal purpose.

The call of God confronts at a place and time of His choosing as we lead our normal lives. We will, however, be required to make choices that are consistent with it when confronted with it. This statement from Paul confirms this:

"But when God, who set me apart from my mother's womb and called me by his grace, was pleased to reveal his Son in me so that I might preach him among the Gentiles, my immediate response was not to consult any human being" (Galatians 1:15-16).

There are seven main invitations we will receive. I want us to look at them one by one, in greater detail, and trace their progression form eternity to time and back to eternity till we are 100 percent conformed to His image. Let's examine them.

Chapter 6

Response and Conformation

As we respond to the different types of calls, we are conformed to the image His Son.

1. The call to salvation conforms us to the image of His Son.

"Fight the good fight of the faith. Take hold of the eternal life to which you were called when you made your good confession in the presence of many witnesses" (1 Timothy 6:12).

The first invitation you will receive from God is a call to be saved, or eternal life. Paul said, "Take hold of the eternal life, to which you were also called." That is the first invitation card. It's the first step to a transformed life. My journey to become a born-again Christian was an interesting one.

When I was young, I used to attend church every Sunday with my parents, but I was not born again. Time and again I heard sermons about being born again, but I refused to heed to the call of God. I was the kind of person the Scripture describes in Proverbs:

"Repent at my rebuke! Then I will pour out my thoughts to you, I will make known to you my teachings. But since you refuse to listen when I call and no one pays attention when I stretch out my hand, since you disregard all my advice and do not accept my rebuke" (Proverbs 1:23-25).

I was refusing to positively respond to the invitation to be saved.

My Experience with Death

I even had a supernatural encounter where I died one night in my sleep. I was ill at that time. I saw my spirit come out of my body, and I could see my body lying lifeless on the bed.

A huge, dark image stood in my room. As soon as I came out, he grabbed me by the hand. His hand was like a vice. Now I understand that being to be death. Death is a condition and a spirit. When you don't know Jesus and you die, he comes to receive your soul and hands you over to hell. That's why Jesus said,

"Very truly I tell you, whoever obeys my word will never see death" (John 8:51).

The ground opened and we descended down a shaft into the earth. As we walked down this tunnel, I begged to be released, but he said nothing. Suddenly I felt the tunnel getting warmer and warmer, and there in the far distance I could see fire and faintly hear people screaming. I knew we were headed for hell. All my pleas to be released fell on deaf ears. Suddenly a voice boomed in the tunnel, "Leave that boy alone. Let's give him a second chance." It was the voice of God.

Immediately death's grip loosened and my soul flew down the tunnel and then out. When I arrived in my room, I jumped into my body, and that was when I came back to life. Can you imagine I still did not give my life to Christ after this terrifying experience? I just lay low for some days and went back to my old ways.

What finally changed me was the preaching of God's Word. One morning a young final-year medical student named Dag Heward-Mills, who was my sister's fiancée, walked into my house and preached Christ to me. On that day I gave my life to Jesus and I have never turned back. This was how I responded to my first call, the call to salvation. The process of transforming into His image had been initialised. This immediately brought me face-to-face with my next call.

2. The call to be holy conforms us to the image of His Son.

"To the church of God in Corinth, to those sanctified in Christ Jesus and called to be his holy people, together with all those everywhere who call on the name of our Lord Jesus Christ—their Lord and ours" (1 Corinthians 1:2).

After I gave my life to Christ, I immediately received my next invitation. It was an invitation to be "holy." I want you to notice, this call is for "all those everywhere who call on the name of our Lord Jesus Christ—their Lord and ours." This is a universal call; no one can exempt this call.

The word saint means holy. If you are called to be a saint, it means you have received an invitation to be holy. You must respond to this invitation positively because it's yet another step to being conformed to the image of Christ.

I thought about all the vices I had to stop. One thing that bothered me the most was separating myself from friends who were unbelievers. I knew a certain type of close association with them would not help me to be a good Christian. Some people are not able to accept this call because of this very reason and the pleasures of sin. Abraham underwent a similar test when God called him. He had to leave some unhelpful relationships.

"The LORD had said to Abram, "Go from your country, your people and your father's household to the land I will show you" (Genesis 12:1).

The Call to Be Holy Is Very Important

To me, the call to salvation and the call to be holy are the most important calls. You can get to heaven without responding to the call to the ministry, but you cannot get to heaven without these two.

In one scenario in heaven, which was painted by Jesus, some ministers of God were turned away at the gates. Jesus said,

"Not everyone who says to me, 'Lord, Lord,' will enter the kingdom of heaven, but only the one who does the will of my Father who is in heaven. Many will say to me on that day, 'Lord, Lord, did we not prophesy in your name and in your name drive out demons and in your name perform many miracles?' Then I will tell them plainly, 'I never knew you. Away from me, you evildoers!' " (Matthew 7:21-23).

You will notice these were people who had responded to the call to ministry. There were famous prophets and miracle workers amongst them. They prophesied and cast out devils. Some did mighty works. Maybe they built huge auditoriums, had great crusades, or performed miracles. There was one slight problem; they had placed the call to ministry above the call to be holy. In this modern world, I see many place more emphasis on achievements than on holiness.

In our own eyes our works are a testament to us that God is with us more than what the Bible says. If you are to choose between the call to ministry and the call to holiness, I advise you to choose the latter. We give more honour to gifted and powerful people and give little regard to their lifestyle. Let's remember the words of Jesus:

"He said to them, 'You are the ones who justify yourselves in the eyes of others, but God knows your hearts. What people value highly is detestable in God's sight' " (Luke 16:15).

It takes sacrifice to respond to the call to be holy.

The call to be holy can only be achieved on the altar of sacrifice. Without sacrifice, you cannot be holy.

My Temptation in London

Years ago when I was a teenager, I visited London on holidays. I decided to fellowship with a local church. One day one of the nice girls in the church suggested to me that we go for a romantic weekend somewhere and have a nice time. She offered to pay the bills. Because I was a serious Christian, I declined. I was able to decline because I decided to sacrifice fleshy and worldly pleasures. This would not have been possible if I had not decided to sacrifice.

Sin is on the increase because many are failing to respond to the call to be a saint. Divorce is on the increase and children are rebelling against parents because of the failure to be saints. Are you one of them?

"Therefore, I urge you, brothers and sisters, in view of God's mercy, to offer your bodies as a living sacrifice, holy and pleasing to God—this is your true and proper worship" (Romans 12:1).

I want you to notice that the word "living sacrifice" comes before "holy". This means you can't be holy without sacrifice. It's also living, because once you are alive you will continue to sacrifice.

3. The call to suffer conforms us to the image of His Son.

"To this you were called, because Christ suffered for you, leaving you an example, that you should follow in his steps. 'He committed no sin, and no deceit was found in his mouth.' When they hurled their insults at him, he did not retaliate; when he suffered, he made no threats. Instead, he entrusted himself to him who judges justly" (1 Peter 2:21-23).

The invitation to be holy logically takes us to the call to suffer. You will suffer if you decide to lead a holy life.

When I was in university I used to have this lecturer who did not like me because I was a very serious Christian. This became worse when he learnt I was also pastoring a small church on Sundays.

He was not concerned about my other mates, who used to go clubbing during the weekends. In fact, sometimes he invited some of them over to his house for drinks. He really persecuted me. One day he told me in private that he would do all he could to stop me from graduating unless I stopped pastoring. His threats kept on ringing in my ears. I suffered emotionally and mentally. By God's grace I was able to complete my architectural course, in spite of his threats and machinations.

Obedience to God can be costly and may entail suffering.

Sometimes Christians can become victims in an office or family environment. They are sometimes persecuted for their faith and consequently have to suffer many things because of that. I have even seen parents persecute their own children, or spouses persecute each other because of Christ. Peter made it clear that suffering is part of our calling:

"To this you were called, because Christ suffered for you, leaving you an example, that you should follow in his steps."

Nowadays Christians see suffering as an attack of the enemy. Not all suffering is an attack. Christ-like qualities like humility, long-suffering, and patience are often produced in the soil of suffering.

Jesus Suffered for His Obedience

Jesus was reviled by the thief on the cross during His crucifixion, but He did not respond with insults. Rather, He committed His case to God and endured. That's why He did not take matters into His own hands.

"When they hurled their insults at him, he did not retaliate; when he suffered, he made no threats. Instead, he entrusted himself to him who judges justly."

The temptation to pay people in their own coin when you feel you have been unfairly treated can be very strong in times of crisis, but that is when our light must shine. "Be not overcome of evil, but overcome evil with good" (Romans 12:21, KJV).

Sometimes married people may not speak to each other for days because they are waiting to see who will break the ice. Now that is pride. To resolve the issue, you must swallow your pride and endure humility to restore the relationship.

Remember that suffering is part of life. Anyone who thinks Christianity does not entail suffering has an unrealistic view of life. Any type of Christianity that excludes suffering is not true Christianity. Consider this statement of Jesus:

"Then he said to them all: 'Whoever wants to be my disciple must deny themselves and take up their cross daily and follow me. For whoever wants to save their life will lose it, but whoever loses their life for me will save it' " (Luke 9:23-24).

To follow Jesus you must deny yourself of your pride, ego, sin, etc., and take up your cross. This is not a literal cross; the cross is a symbol of pain. It's painful to look into the eyes of someone you love but is not born again and say, "Baby, I love you, but the Word of God prevents me from marrying an unbeliever."

The emotional pain that comes from denying yourself is the cross. The cross is the pain you feel when you deny yourself of something for the sake of Christ. It's painful to apologise; it's painful to say no to something that is nice but wrong. It can be painful to forgive, but that's the cross. Someone said, your cross is where your will and God's will cross.

What type of suffering qualifies as Christian suffering?

Not all suffering can be described as Christian suffering. Christian suffering has unique features. Let's examine some.

"If you are insulted because of the name of Christ, you are blessed, for the Spirit of glory and of God rests on you. If you suffer, it should not be as a murderer or thief or any other kind of criminal, or even as a meddler. However, if you suffer as a Christian, do not be ashamed, but praise God that you bear that name" (1 Peter 4:14-16).

This verse contrasts Christian suffering with suffering for wrongdoing. Here are a few differences.

The first is motivation. The motivation of Christian suffering is for the "name of Christ" or for the "glory" or praise of God. This means you are suffering because of Christ and His Word.

Secondly, Christian suffering has no evil associations. When you suffer as a Christian, you don't suffer because you have done evil. Rather, you suffer for obeying the Word of God. Suffering the repercussions of wrongdoing is not Christian suffering. That's punishment.

Sometimes you can have married Christian couples whose spouses deny them sex or money, yet they remain faithful because of God's Word. That's Christian suffering.

This type of suffering is key if you are to develop the image of God. When you refuse to suffer and take the law into your hands, it will prevent you from transforming into His image.

4. The call to be blessed conforms us to the image of His Son.

"Do not repay evil with evil or insult with insult. On the contrary, repay evil with blessing, because to this you were called so that you may inherit a blessing" (1 Peter 3:9).

Sometimes when my children don't want to study, I say to them, "As for suffering, you will suffer. The only thing you can do is to choose the type of suffering. You can choose the suffering of studying to be an engineer or the suffering of being a labourer on a building site." When you are afraid of suffering, you will not do well in anything, because everything, from a good marriage, to a good job, to serving God, to finances, will include suffering if you are to excel. That's why following the will of God in obedience with its attendant suffering automatically brings you to the call to be blessed.

Years ago when I was in my teens I took a stroll with a friend of mine in my neighbourhood.

We came across a mutual female friend of ours and he invited her to a party he was organising. When he gave her the card she said, "Eii Joe, I know you have wicked plans for me." She declined. I find the response of the girl still funny up to this day. The girl felt there was something sinister about the invitation. Many think there is something sinister about the call of God.

I was afraid I would not be blessed if I answered the call of God.

One thing that kept me from being born again when I was younger was the thought that behind God's invitation was a sinister plan. I was afraid He would destroy my life and I would be miserable if I responded to the call to salvation. The devil tells people the call of God is for poor, unintelligent, weak, and frustrated people with problems they cannot solve, so they run to God for solace.

The devil has sold this lie to many. He has told them if you serve the Lord, you will be unhappy and poor. Worse of all, He will give you someone to marry who is boring and you don't love.

I was afraid I would become a poor pastor living in some outlandish place. I was afraid the Lord would give me an "ugly" wife I did not like, even though beauty is relative. I believe everyone is beautiful.

The devil told me it was an invitation to destroy my life. Because of this, I hardened my heart. This is not true, because God created man to bless him. The story of Adam and Eve corroborates this.

The call of God is designed to bless you.

"God blessed them and said to them, 'Be fruitful and increase in number; fill the earth and subdue it. Rule over the fish in the sea and the birds in the sky and over every living creature that moves on the ground' " (Genesis 1:28).

I have experienced the blessing of God as I have responded to the several invitations I have received from Him.

My Testimony About the Blessing of God

The first blessing is that I am saved and following God's plan for my life to the best of my ability. Even if I am wrong, at least I am sincerely wrong. May the Lord have mercy on me!

Secondly I have a wonderful wife whom I love and four beautiful kids. Our home has been an oasis of unbroken peace and love for the past twenty-five years since we married. By the grace of God I have not had a disagreement with my wife overnight over all these years.

God has anointed me to do His work and gifted me with unusual gifts and a wonderful ministry. It's a privilege to serve Him. Financially I am okay and cannot be described as poor by any definition. My house has been blessed with good health. I owe no man anything but love. It's my prayer I continue to walk with Him. I can truly say I am a blessed person. I want to thank God for the invitations and for giving me the grace to RSVP them. I give Him the glory. I say this not to boast, but to testify and encourage someone that it's good to respond to the call of God.

God called Abraham to bless him; not to curse him. I believe that will be your story too. He said to him, "I will make you into a great nation, and I will bless you; I will make your name great, and you will be a blessing" (Genesis 12:2).

5. The call to ministry conforms us to the image of His Son.

The call to ministry is an invitation to help God in His agenda of winning souls and transforming them into the image of His Son.

I believe every Christian has been called to ministry. This does not mean every Christian will be a full-time priest, but it means everyone should be involved in the work of the Lord one way or the other. Some people may do great things and some may do minor things, depending on their individual calling. Some may be full time, some part, etc.

In the list of great Old Testament saints in the book of Hebrews, you will see ordinary people like Rahab the harlot standing toe to toe with giants like Abraham:

"By faith the prostitute Rahab, because she welcomed the spies, was not killed with those who were disobedient" (Hebrews 11:31).

"By faith Abraham, when called to go to a place he would later receive as his inheritance, obeyed and went, even though he did not know where he was going. By faith he made his home in the promised land like a stranger in a foreign country; he lived in tents, as did Isaac and Jacob, who were heirs with him of the same promise" (Hebrews 11:8-9).

Someone once asked me, "How can I know what God wants me to do?" I replied, "Embrace the first opportunity to do something for God. God will arrange the rest." Rahab just took the opportunity that was presented to her, according to her strength and ability, and she is mentioned with Abraham.

"Each of you should use whatever gift you have received to serve others, as faithful stewards of

God's grace in its various forms. If anyone speaks, they should do so as one who speaks the very words of God. If anyone serves, they should do so with the strength God provides, so that in all things God may be praised through Jesus Christ. To him be the glory and the power for ever and ever. Amen" (1 Peter 4:10-11).

The Responsibility of Every Believer

After being saved, you have a responsibility to minister or serve others spiritually. Ephesians describes this ministry in greater detail.

"So Christ himself gave the apostles, the prophets, the evangelists, the pastors and teachers, to equip his people for works of service, so that the body of Christ may be built up until we all reach unity in the faith and in the knowledge of the Son of God and become mature, attaining to the whole measure of the fullness of Christ" (Ephesians 4:11-13).

I want you to notice the following.

God gave the primary ministry gifts of apostles, prophets, evangelists, pastors, and teachers for the perfection or spiritual maturing of saints. Note, not church members, but saints. When you are not a saint, it's difficult to grow or mature spiritually. The aim of this spiritual growth is to equip them to participate in "works of service."

Church is not just a place to be blessed; it's also a place to serve.

The primary work of all Christians is to witness to others. That's why Jesus said to His disciples, "Go into all the world and preach the gospel to all creation. Whoever believes and is baptized will be saved, but whoever does not believe will be condemned" (Mark 16:15-16).

This is not the only thing Christians can do. There are other things like counselling, ushering, singing, etc. We must allow the Holy Spirit to guide us into His will.

I want you to notice the ultimate aim of ministry. It is to help transform others to "the whole measure of the fullness of Christ." This means that the ultimate aim of all forms of ministry, be it apostle, prophet, or teacher, is to transform believers into the image of Christ. We must be concerned when the people we minister to are not changed into His image, but into something else. Are we missing the point?

6. The call to glory conforms us to the image of His Son.

"encouraging, comforting and urging you to live lives worthy of God, who calls you into his kingdom and glory" (1 Thessalonians 2:12).

My Dad Was Called to Glory

My dad lived up to ninety years before he was called to glory; he died. The death of a Christian is not a call to damnation, but a call to glory, or beauty. The call to glory happens when God calls you home.

My father died as a committed Christian. I remember sitting by his bedside as he lay dying. I asked him, "What do you see?" He replied, "I see people preparing for something like a party, and it seems they are waiting for someone." I believe he was in transition and saw the saints in glory preparing to meet him. A couple of days later, after his dinner, he prayed and closed his eyes; he was gone. He was called "unto His kingdom and glory." Glory, because our bodies and everything will eventually change into something more beautiful and superior.

"The sun has one kind of splendor, the moon another and the stars another; and star differs from star in splendor. So will it be with the resurrection of the dead. The body that is sown is perishable, it is raised imperishable" (1 Corinthians 15:41-42).

Chapter 7

The Marriage Feast of the Lamb

The call to the marriage feast is a unique call and different from the others in purpose. First of all, it's the only call that does not have the purpose of conforming us to the image of Jesus. We would have been resurrected and reunited with Christ. This is because at this time all God's children would have been fully conformed to the image of Jesus.

Secondly, this call takes place in heaven; not the earth.

Thirdly, the purpose of this call seems to be to reward us and give us some privileges in heaven. This will be based on how we led our lives and served the Lord on earth.

Finally, the most striking thing about the call to the feast is: Not all Christians in heaven can attend this feast because it's an invitation-only feast. What are the qualifications for this feast?

I want to present different accounts of this same feast from different books in the Bible. The books of the Bible can act like video cameras. They record from different angles, so they can provide different accounts of the same story. You have to put them together to form a full picture.

The first account of this feast is taken from the book of Revelation.

"Let us rejoice and be glad and give him glory! For the wedding of the Lamb has come, and his bride has made herself ready. Fine linen, bright and clean, was given her to wear. (Fine linen stands for the righteous acts of God's holy people.) Then the angel said to me, 'Write this: Blessed are those who are invited to the wedding supper of the Lamb!' And he added, 'These are the true words of God' " (Revelation 19:7-9).

This feast takes place in heaven, and it seems not everyone in heaven is invited to this feast because, "Blessed are those who are invited to the wedding supper of the Lamb!"

What are the qualifications for attending the marriage supper of the Lamb?

1. You have to be saved and be in heaven.

First of all, it is called the "wedding supper of the Lamb" and it's for the bride of Christ, the church.

2. You have to be invited.

"Blessed are they which are called unto the marriage supper of the Lamb."

It's an invitation-only supper; not all are invited. It's for a select few.

3. You need to be in the appropriate attire or garment to be at the feast.

"Fine linen, bright and clean, was given her to wear." We are told, "Fine linen stands for the righteous acts of God's holy people."

It seems the clothes will be made of a fabric of "holy works." I suspect our works for the Lord will determine the amount of material available for the gown. If this proves to be the case, those who did very little for the Lord when they were on earth may be in bikinis because they will have very little material.

What will happen if you don't have the appropriate attire?

As the feast progressed, the Lord came round to fraternise with the guests. Suddenly He saw someone in appropriate attire. Look at what happened.

"But when the king came in to see the guests, he noticed a man there who was not wearing wedding clothes. He asked, 'How did you get in here without wedding clothes, friend?' The man was speechless. Then the king told the attendants, 'Tie him hand and foot, and throw him outside, into the darkness, where there will be weeping and gnashing of teeth.' For many are invited, but few are chosen" (Matthew 22:11-14).

The Lord saw a man in inappropriate clothing. He was in heaven all right, and a child of God, but he was not supposed to be at the feast because he had not been invited or called to the feast.

I guess his works on the earth were insufficient to earn him a place at the table. He was cast out into outer darkness. Then the King made a profound statement, "Many are called but few are chosen."

This means many will be called to heaven, but few will be chosen to attend this banquet. It's my prayer that you and I meet at the table. We will be jockeying for positions with great people like John Wesley, the apostle Paul, and others. The uninvited guest was cast into outer darkness.

Faith is an example of the righteous work of the saints.

Jesus made a related comment concerning this same feast when He healed the centurion servant. He was amazed at his faith because he told Him he did not need Jesus to come to his house to heal his servant. He believed a word from Him would be enough.

"When Jesus heard this, he was amazed and said to those following him, 'Truly I tell you, I have not found anyone in Israel with such great faith. I say to you that many will come from the east and the west, and will take their places at the feast with Abraham, Isaac and Jacob in the kingdom of heaven. But the subjects of the kingdom will be thrown outside, into the darkness, where there will be weeping and gnashing of teeth' " (Matthew 8:10-12).

Abraham, Isaac, and Jacob, the patriarchs, are mentioned as being present, so obviously the scene is heaven. Jesus commented that people who were not Jews, like the centurion, would be invited to this feast because of their works of faith. Once again He repeated that the children or subjects of the Kingdom are not unbelievers, but children of the Kingdom will be cast into outer darkness. Why were some cast into outer darkness, and what is it?

What Is Outer Darkness? The Vision

One day I had a vision and found myself in heaven. I visited a large mansion, which was under construction. It was too beautiful; the floors were made of different colours of marble beyond description. An angel took me for a tour.

I asked who the house was for and I was told it was for Jackie, one of our Sunday school teachers.

I inquired why it was not finished. I was informed that our works on earth add to the construction and beauty of the house, so construction ends when you die. Jesus once had a conversation with His disciples about mansions in heaven. This is what He said.

There Are Unfinished Mansions in Heaven

"My Father's house has many rooms; if that were not so, would I have told you that I am going there to prepare a place for you?" (John 14:2).

The mansions of heaven are still under construction. "I go to prepare a place for you." What mighty mansions they will be. I shudder to think about the size of God's own mansion, because these mansions are in His house. I have the game Monopoly, and all the houses and hotels in the game are in my house. My children used to have toy houses, and they were all in my house. The mansions of this world are like toy houses in God's house.

The Man from Outer Darkness

As we continued the tour, we came across someone who had tears in his eyes. He was dressed in white, but only his clothes did not glow or shine much like some of the people I had seen earlier. I asked, "Why is this man weeping?" because

I thought there was no weeping in heaven. He said, "There is weeping, but of a different sort." He drew my attention to a scene in the book of Revelation, where John was found weeping in heaven.

"Then I saw in the right hand of him who sat on the throne a scroll with writing on both sides and sealed with seven seals. And I saw a mighty angel proclaiming in a loud voice, 'Who is worthy to break the seals and open the scroll?' I wept and wept because no one was found who was worthy to open the scroll or look inside" (Revelation 5:1-2, 4).

Can There Be Weeping in Heaven?

The scene of this account is heaven, yet John was found weeping, because no man was found worthy to open the book in the hand of the Lord. How come he was able to weep in heaven when there is supposed to be no weeping in heaven? He wept because of the inability to open the book.

I asked, "What type of weeping is found in heaven?" He said, "The difference is, the people don't weep because of pain, sorrow, and death. They weep because they feel they could have done more for the Lord when they were on earth, and there is no pain associated with it." Any form of weeping caused by death or sorrow cannot be found in heaven. But weeping because of the inability to do something seems to be possible.

"He will wipe every tear from their eyes. There will be no more death or mourning or crying or pain, for the old order of things has passed away" (Revelation 21:4).

The Outer Part of the City

He continued, "This man is weeping because he lives at an area of heaven called outer darkness, and it's at the outer part of the city." He continued, "People who live there can only visit the inner part, but can't stay there."

It's like being on a plane. You can visit someone in the first class cabin, but you can't sit there. You have to go back to economy if you have an economy seat.

I asked, "But why the connotation of darkness?" He smiled and said, "Because your works determine your clothes and the kind of glory or light that is emitted from them. The more your works, the brighter the glory. Most of the people who live there did not do much for the Lord, so that part of the city looks darker compared to the glory of the center. That's why it's called outer darkness."

In the book of Daniel, it is stated that our works for the Lord will determine our glory.

Daniel described why some Christians will shine more than others.

"Multitudes who sleep in the dust of the earth will awake: some to everlasting life, others to shame and everlasting contempt. Those who are wise will shine like the brightness of the heavens, and those who lead many to righteousness, like the stars for ever and ever" (Daniel 12:2-3).

There is a distinction made between three classes of people in this verse. The first is those who will be resurrected to shame and everlasting contempt; that's unbelievers. Secondly, those who will resurrect to "everlasting life." That's believers. Thirdly, believers who won souls to Christ; "They that turn many to righteousness."

Amongst believers, some will shine more or have greater glory. This will be determined by our works. Believers who won souls or turned many to righteousness will shine more or have more glory than those who have little works.

Final Words

Friend, life is short, and it continues after death. There is a reason why you are alive on the earth. It's time to respond to the INVITATION and be conformed to the image of His Son.

If you don't know Jesus as your personal Lord and saviour, now is a good opportunity to respond to the call to salvation.

You can pray this prayer with me if you want to follow Jesus.

Dear Lord, today I repent of my sins. I believe that You died for me. Please wash away my sins with Your blood. Come and live in my heart and be the Lord of my life. Help me to serve You all the days of my life. Thank You, Jesus, for coming into my heart.

If you prayed this simple prayer with faith and sincerity, it means you have responded to the first call. Find a good Bible-believing church to attend, so you can grow spiritually.

If God gives me life and grace and Jesus tarries, I will be writing the sequel to this book, *Manifestation*. I will be looking at practical ways to manifest your calling. Stay tuned.

"Therefore, my brothers and sisters, make every effort to confirm your calling and election. For if you do these things, you will never stumble, and you will receive a rich welcome into the eternal kingdom of our Lord and Savior Jesus Christ" (2 Peter 1:10-11).

Thanks for reading and God bless you.

Kakra Baiden

About the Author

Kakra Baiden

Many years ago the Lord Jesus Christ appeared in a vision to Kakra Baiden and called him into the ministry as a prophet, teacher, and miracle worker. He is also known as "the walking Bible" for his supernatural ability to preach and teach the Bible from memory.

Pastor Baiden is an architect by profession and serves as a bishop of the Lighthouse Chapel International denomination. He has trained many pastors and planted many churches within the Lighthouse denomination.

Currently he is the senior pastor of the Morning Star Cathedral, Lighthouse Chapel International, Accra. He is a sought-after revivalist and conference speaker.

He is also the president of Airpower, a ministry through which he touches the world through radio and TV broadcasts, books, CDs, videos, the Internet, and international conferences dubbed "The Airpower Conference." He has ministered the Word on every continent and is also the author of the best-selling book, *Squatters*.

Pastor Baiden is married to Lady Rev. Dr. Ewuradwoa Baiden and they have four children.

For additional information on Kakra Baiden's books and messages (CDs and DVDs), write to any of these addresses:

US

26219 Halbrook Glen Lane
Katy, TX 77494

UK

32 Tern Road
Hampton, Hargate
Cambridgeshire
Pe78DG

GHANA

P.O. Box SK 1067
Sakumono Estates, Tema
Ghana-West Africa

E-MAIL: info@kakrabaiden.org

WEBSITE: www.kakrabaiden.org

FACEBOOK: www.facebook.com/KakraBaiden

TWITTER: www.twitter.com/ProphetKakraB

CONTACT NUMBERS:

+233 273 437 440 / +233 249 217 272 /
+233 207575215